THE WRITER'S BLOCK WORKBOOK

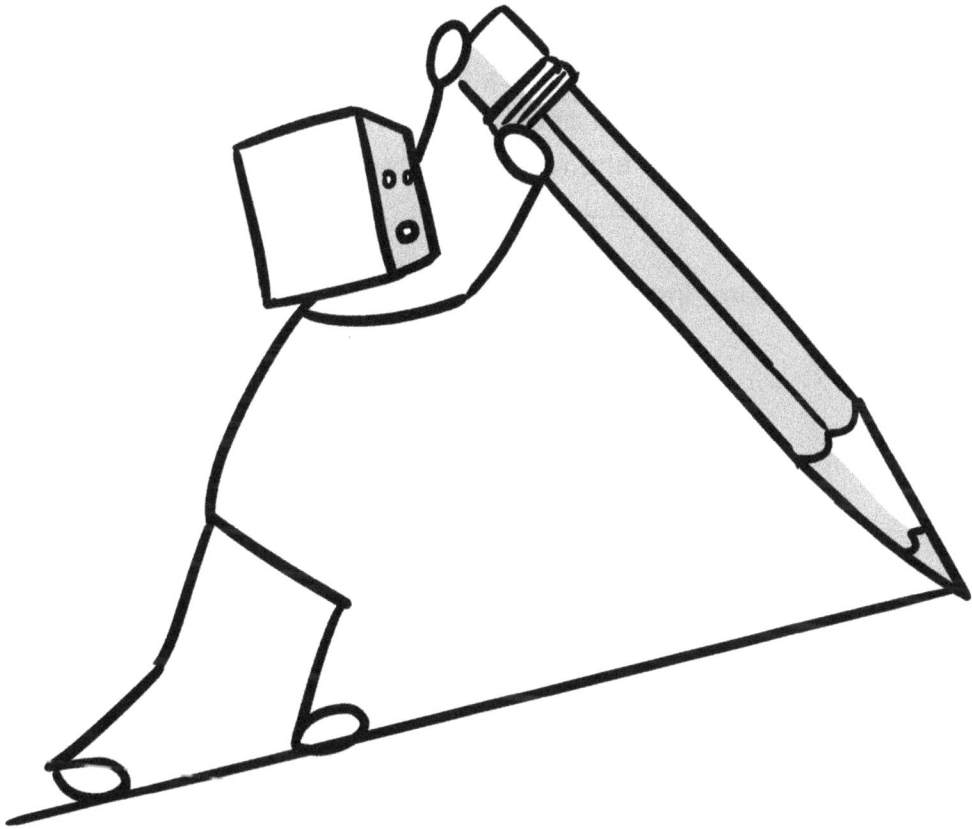

A PSYCHOLOGIST'S GUIDE FOR WORKING WITH AND THROUGH WRITER'S BLOCK

For bulk purchases and/or institutional discounts, contact Empress Publications through www.empresspublications.com.

EMPRESS

PUBLICATIONS

WWW.EMPRESSPUBLICATIONS.COM

"Unfortunately, many people suffer from BPS—Blank Page Syndrome. Let's face it: starting to write is scary. Seeing the cursor blinking at you on that bright white screen, realizing that you now have to come up with three or ten or twenty pages of text all on your own—it's enough to give anyone a major case of writer's block!"

—Stefanie Weisman

———————————

This book is dedicated to any writer who's ever suffered from BPS, who's come down with a case of writer's block.

Which means it's dedicated to every writer ever.

INTRODUCTION

"Writer's block is going to happen to you. You will read what little you've written lately and see with absolute clarity that it is total dog shit. . . . Or else you haven't been able to write anything at all for a while. The fear that you'll never write again is going to hit you when you feel not only lost and unable to find a few little bread crumbs that would identify the path you were on but also when you're at the lowest ebb of energy and faith."

~Anne Lamott
Bird By Bird: Some Instructions on Writing and Life

The Oxford Languages Dictionary defines writer's block as "the condition of being unable to think of what to write or how to proceed with writing." Merriam-Webster defines the condition as "a psychological inhibition preventing a writer from proceeding with a piece," I suppose in contradistinction from a physical inhibition like being in a coma, though writer's block can often feel just like that—a coma from which we fear we'll never wake and write again. Fear not—Dictionary.com calls writer's block "a usually temporary condition in which a writer finds it impossible to proceed with the writing of a novel, play, or other work."

Whew. Inevitable, according to Anne Lamott, but usually temporary, according to Dictionary.com. Since the latter has all the words, let's go with that definition!

I have been writing ever since I was a wee child, nearly six decades now, and I've experienced my share of writer's block. In fact, the idea for writing this book came out of my current state of writer's block on another book-in-progress for which I fear the term "total dog shit" may be apropos. (Well, not total dog shit. Just dog shit.)

It was, ironically, when I experienced my worst case of writer's block—writing my dissertation for a PhD in psychology—that I became interested in the psychology of writer's block. And in the intervening twenty years, I've learned that no matter how much I understand my writer's block psychologically, in the words of the immortal Alanis Morrisette, "the only way out is through, the only way you'll feel better." So this book is an invitation—let's go through it, together, until we find our way out.

Conventional wisdom says the way out of writing block is simple—you just write. It's a twist on this Vincent van Gogh quote: "If you hear a voice within you saying: You are no painter, then paint by all means, lad, and that voice will be silenced, but only by working." And so it goes—if we hear a voice telling us we are no writer, or we are only a writer of total dog shit, then we should write, by all means, and that voice will be silenced. Louis L'Amour, prolific American writer of 105 novels, short-story collections, and nonfiction books, admonishes us to do the same: "Start writing, no matter what. The water does not flow until the faucet is turned on."

Just turn the faucet on, lad. Just turn the faucet on. Sounds so easy, right? And yet for those of us who have experienced sometimes debilitating writer's block, there's no way we can just turn the faucet on—it's like all of our fingers are superglued together inside oven mitts wrapped in our granny's thick quilt and tied behind our backs with industrial-strength duct tape. Just turn the faucet on, just sit down and start pecking away at the piece we're stuck on, word by word (or bird by bird, as Anne Lamott's father suggests)—that's not always helpful advice.

If that worked, you wouldn't need this book.

This book is inspired by an idea from Jane Anne Staw's excellent book (bible?) *Unstuck: A Supportive and Practical Guide to Working Through Writer's Block*. She writes, "Whatever we do to overcome a writing block, it should involve taking a direction in which we have not headed before. Doing more of the same—avoiding, criticizing, blaming, beating up on ourselves—is certain to lead to failure. Hope often lies in taking a different route, or at least an unexpected turn. . . . Interrupting our habitual series of behaviors and responses toward writing gives us a chance to open ourselves to new reactions and attitudes."

And that's why you need this book. Because it is important to write your way *out* of writer's block by writing your way *through* writer's block, but often that's best served by taking a different route, approaching writing from a different direction. So this book seeks to offer you a way to interrupt those habits that led to your writer's block in the first place, and develop some new reactions and attitudes toward your writing self to break through your psychological inhibitions and make writer's block a temporary condition.

All as you continue to write. To write right in this workbook, to keep working at writing, as van Gogh would admonish his lad, if his lad were a writer and not a painter.

Can I promise you that if you make your way through this workbook, you'll bust your way out of your writer's block? No, of course not. I don't even suggest you use it that way, moving through it page by page, dutifully doing all the exercises. I suggest you use it instead as a way to prime the pump, to get the flow going, to acknowledge both that you're blocked and you're working your way through the block. Open it to any page before you begin a writing session, or flip through it randomly and do the exercises that call to you that day.

And while I can't promise your block will be eviscerated, dynamited into a million little pieces by any one—or all—of the exercises in this book, I hope that this book will

- Normalize writing block
- Engender hope that it can—and will—be moved through with effort and attention
- Offer at every unexpected turn an inroad leading to a deeper understanding of the psychological inhibitions contributing to your writer's block
- Illustrate that we can take writer's block seriously while also having some fun with it

It is this last hope behind the whimsical images of the writer with a block head created by illustrator Muhammad Wachid Khoirul (check out his work on Fiverr under the handle "mwkhoirul"). Yes, writer's block is a god who must be honored and propitiated, a devil who must be defanged and decloaked, and an erstwhile angel mediating between the two, but it's also a trickster with no need to be treated too reverently. So into the soup of this book, I've poured some fun and games to keep it light, because let's face it, writer's block is a heavy enough meal already. Or, to use another metaphor, the fun and games are the spoonful of sugar making the medicine this book hopes to offer go down, go way way down, until we're standing on the mountaintop, free at last, free at last from (at least this bout of) writer's block.

angry angry waste frustrated overcome stupid block
project help nowhere dry chore page
frustrated brain waste
stuck lost project constipated can't blank critic flow
dead cloudy stuck writer's block never

can't bad
edit bad
nothing chore
constipated dead
help empty
nowhere lost dark
nothing
critic never
page cry brain
tears cry bad
imposter dry cloudy
stupid stupid suffer
brain
waste
chore block
angry cloudy
dry frustration dead staring deflated incomplete neverpage stare
criticism criticism flustration
project writer's block help critic deflated flow ideas
cry words ideas imposter suffer edit anxiety incomplete
incomplete constipated staring lost block criticism nowhere ideas
dark anxiety
empty block criticism
dark writer's block block overcome frustrated can't
flow nothing empty
stuck words imposter blank stare edit

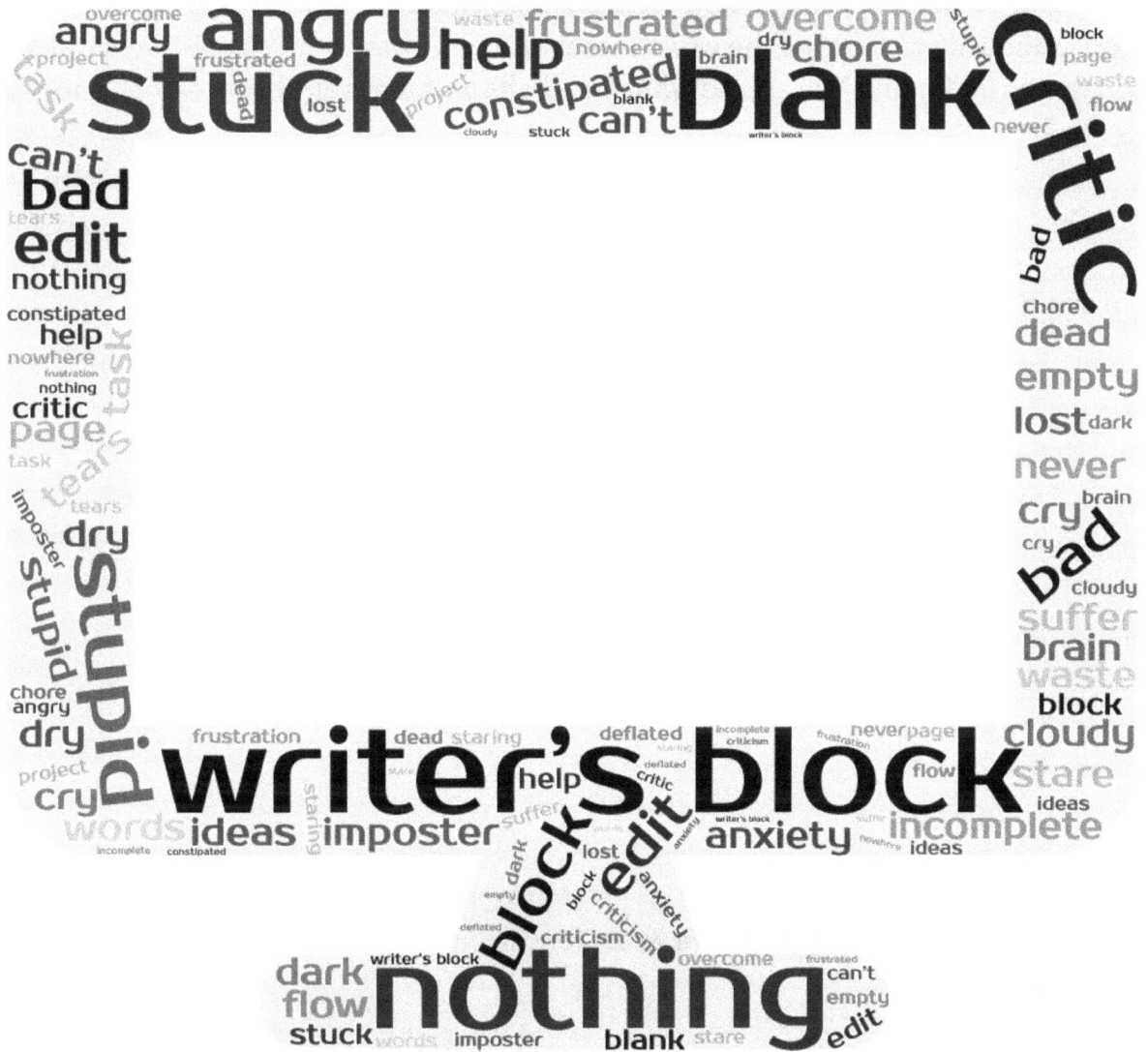

What words jump out at you in your current state of blockage? Highlight them, circle them, cross them out with a big black Sharpie. Add your own words onto the blank screen.

> "I went for years not finishing anything. Because, of course, when you finish something you can be judged."
>
> "All writing problems are psychological problems. Blocks usually stem from the fear of being judged. If you imagine the world listening, you'll never write a line. That's why privacy is so important. You should write first drafts as if they will never be shown to anyone."
>
> ~Erica Jong

I am afraid people will judge my writing as…

I am afraid people will judge me as a writer for…

I am afraid to be judged by…

I've been hurt when my writing was judged by…

Is there anything you can do right now to protect your privacy on this draft you're blocked on?

The Uninspired Writer

C	S	S	P	P	C	L	I	C	H	E	D	S	B
R	U	X	C	E	E	M	P	T	Y	N	D	R	L
Y	O	R	L	E	L	Z	I	L	C	H	P	F	I
T	N	U	N	I	N	S	P	I	R	E	D	B	S
E	I	E	M	L	O	T	R	I	T	E	A	L	T
I	D	H	I	R	O	R	O	P	C	C	T	A	L
X	U	A	M	O	D	D	U	L	L	E	S	N	E
N	T	C	P	I	S	I	E	L	A	T	S	K	S
A	I	K	O	R	D	E	R	O	S	N	E	C	S
Y	T	E	S	E	O	F	E	A	R	F	U	L	D
D	A	Y	T	F	E	E	S	T	U	C	K	L	S
R	L	E	E	N	E	R	C	O	I	D	E	M	E
Y	P	D	R	I	D	U	B	L	O	C	K	E	D
I	D	E	P	R	E	S	S	E	D	T	A	D	M

UNINSPIRED
PLATITUDINOUS
CLICHED
STUCK
DULL
INFERIOR
MEDIOCRE
LISTLESS
DEPRESSED
DRY
HACKEYED
ANXIETY
ZILCH
BLOCKED
IMPOSTER
CENSORED
FEARFUL
TRITE
BLANK
STALE
EMPTY

Find the answer key in the back of the book.

> "A little writer's block can be a good thing. Your inner-literary critic's way of gently letting you know you're really stinking up the joint. You're off track. Lost in the weeds. Need to go back and rethink things."
>
> ~Quentin R. Bufogle

What stinks about your writing or your writing project right now? Note: "Everything" is not an acceptable answer. Be specific—what might you need to go back and rethink?

> "I sit for a moment and then say a small prayer—please help me get out of the way so I can write what wants to be written. Sometimes ritual quiets the racket. Try it. Any number of things may work for you—an altar, for instance, or votive candles, sage smudges. . . . Rituals are a good signal to your unconscious that it is time to kick in."
>
> ~Anne Lamott

What writing rituals do you have?

What writing rituals could you add?

What writing rituals will you add? (Hint: Try one right now!)

"My goal is to write every day. I say it is my ideal. I am careful not to pass judgment or create anxiety if I do not do it. No one lives up to his ideal."

~Natalie Goldberg

What is your writing ideal?

How far away from your ideal are you?

How do you treat yourself and/or talk to yourself when you don't meet your ideal?

> "That's one of the great advantages of age. You can say, I don't want to, I don't care, you can throw temper tantrums, and nobody minds."
>
> ~James Lee Burke

Well, maybe people in your life will mind, but these pages don't. So, have at it. Throw a major temper tantrum. Bitch and whine and moan and groan about just how hard it is to be a writer. Hold nothing back. Be your terrible two-year-old self in full meltdown.

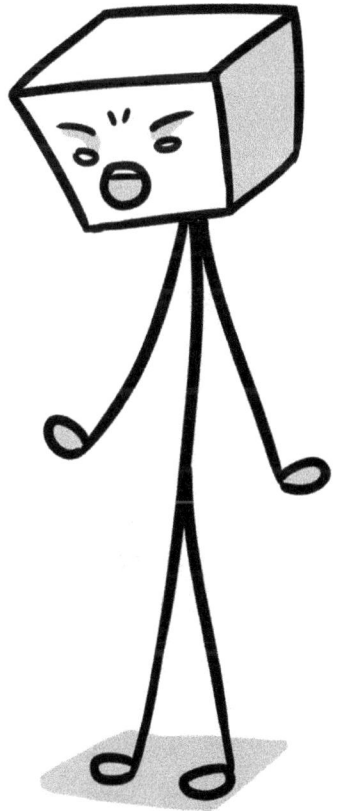

> "Exposure to so much self-abuse from the writers I teach and those I work with has taught me to see writing block as a kind of autoimmune disease, a condition that causes people to turn against themselves and become their own harshest, most relentless critics."
>
> ~Jane Anne Staw

Please check all the boxes that characterize your current condition:

- ☐ Headache
- ☐ Fever
- ☐ Lethargy
- ☐ Agitation
- ☐ Stomach ache
- ☐ Mood swings
- ☐ Constipation
- ☐ Diarrhea
- ☐ Depression
- ☐ Aching muscles
- ☐ Aching heart
- ☐ Excessive sleepiness
- ☐ Anger
- ☐ Sadness
- ☐ Restlessness
- ☐ Loss of appetite
- ☐ Overeating
- ☐ Overdrinking
- ☐ Inability to focus
- ☐ Anxiety
- ☐ Insomnia
- ☐ Irritability
- ☐ Other (please list)

Now, let's play doctor! Write yourself a prescription for whatever would make you feel better.

R
X

NAME_____

ADDRESS_____

_____

_____

Prescription:

Dr. Feelgood

SIGNATURE *Dr. Feelgood*   DATE _____

WRITE BACK!

"Finally, one just has to shut up, sit down, and write. That is painful. Writing is so simple, basic, and austere. There are no fancy gadgets to make it more attractive. Our monkey minds would much rather discuss our resistances with a friend at a lovely restaurant or go to a therapist to work out our writing blocks. We like to complicate simple tasks. There is a Zen saying: 'Talk when you talk, walk when you walk, and die when you die.' Write when you write. Stop battling yourself with guilt, accusations, and strong-arm threats."

~Natalie Goldberg

Dear Natalie,

_____

_____

_____

_____

_____

_____

_____

_____

_____

Your Fellow Writer, Me

In *Unstuck: A Supportive and Practical Guide to Working Through Writer' Block*, Jane Anne Staw talks about the scene of her "first full unblocking"—a local diner where she ordered a cup of coffee, where her writing flowed. Two cups of coffee later, she had four pages of writing. It hits her like epiphany: "The difference between my experience that day in the diner and my usual struggle to write was place. My desk at home was associated with hours of hand-writing attempts to write, with wad after wad of paper I had failed to fill, with hours of disappointment and self-doubt. The diner, on the other hand, held a more positive valence." Her conclusion: "Writing in a place you enjoy can be like soaking up the sun before you dive into the cold waters of a mountain lake."

Where do you usually write? List all the places.

Where do you typically write best?

List of all of the places you enjoy where you could conceivably write.

Make a commitment this week to visit one of those places and give writing a try. Then come back here and write about what happened.

> "Although we seldom talk about it in these terms, writing is a means of prayer. It connects us to the invisible world. It gives us a gate or a conduit for the other world to talk to us whether we call it the subconscious, the unconscious, the superconscious, the imagination, the Muse."
>
> ~Julia Cameron

Write a prayer to your God, gods, angels, spirit guides, power animals, to your subconscious, unconscious, superconscious, to your imagination, your Muse, your higher power, your creative soul, for help in overcoming your writer's block.

"The page is your mirror. What happens inside you is reflected back. You come face-to-face with your own resistance, lack of balance, self-loathing, and insatiable ego—and also with your singular vision, guts, and fortitude."

~Dani Shapiro

What do you see when you look in the mirror at your writer self right now? Draw your own reflection.

FAMOUS AUTHORS

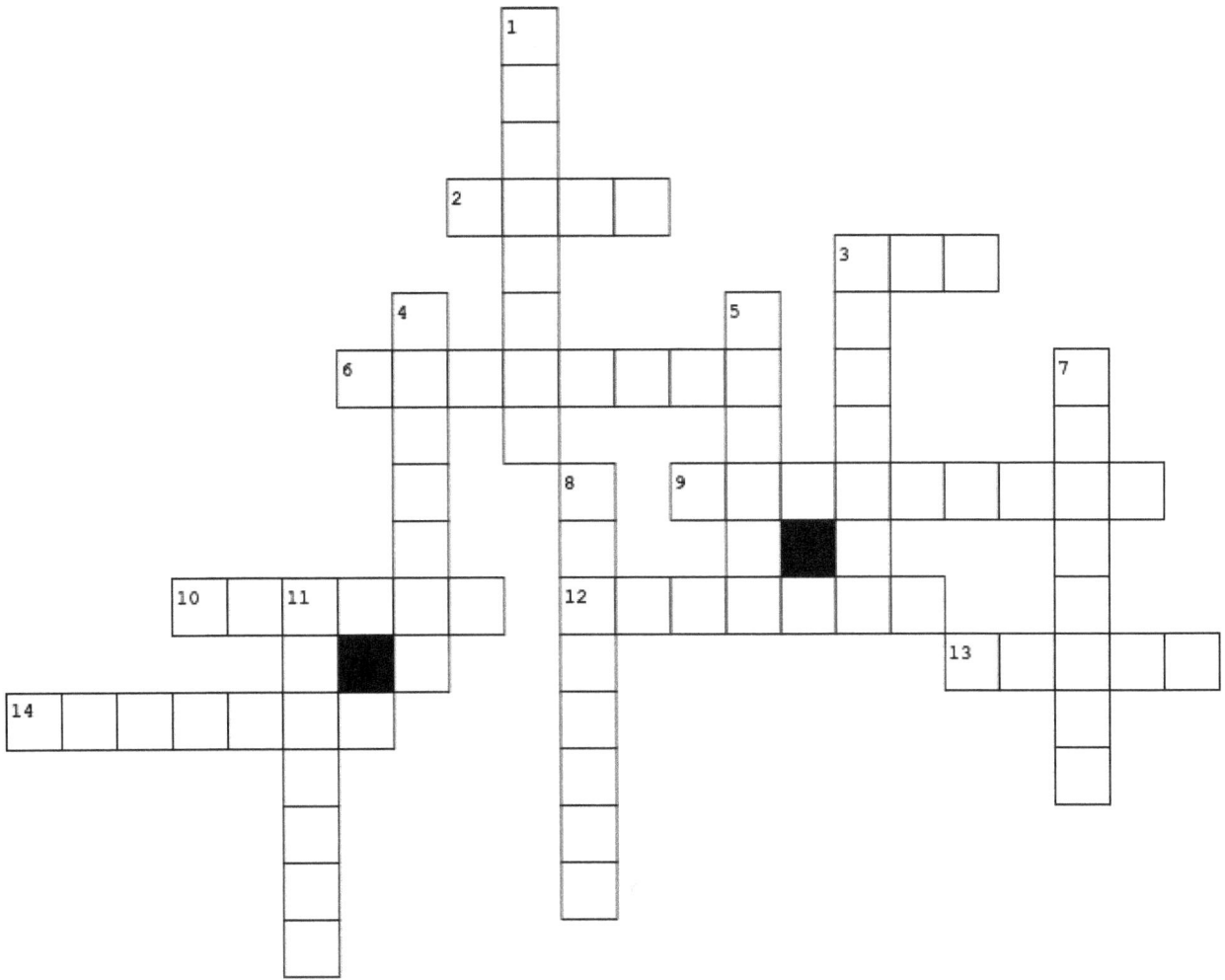

Across

2. Misery loves company
3. You'd feel joy if you joined her lucky club
6. Catch him in the rye
9. Nicknamed Papa
10. Pride or prejudiced?
12. A famous potter maker
13. Red fish blue fish
14. A century of solitude

Down

1. Murder she wrote
3. It's all about the ring
4. Be careful of the fire next time
5. Farm animals
7. Books are burning at 451 degrees
8. She's beloved
11. She created a monster

Find the answer key at the end of the book.

> "To write you must feel safe. Punishment and harshness threaten us, put us at risk. Why would sensible people, knowing that they will be punished if they fail, want to pull up a chair and begin to write? Why would any of us purposefully or deliberately expose ourselves to deprivation? Wouldn't it make more sense to take the opposite approach? To think about the ways we can *entice* ourselves to write—the rewards we can offer ourselves for doing something we do not look forward to doing?"
>
> ~Jane Anne Staw

Let's brainstorm a list of:

Small enticements for small writing projects

Medium enticements for medium writing projects

Large enticements for large writing projects

> "A hammer made of deadlines is the surest tool for crushing writer's block."
>
> ~Ryan Lilly

Here's some common wisdom around working under a deadline. Is there anything new you can try?

- [ ] If you don't have a deadline, give yourself one.
- [ ] Tell someone else about your deadline, and ask them to hold you accountable.
- [ ] Schedule your writing time into your calendar in doable blocks, and show up for yourself on time.
- [ ] Prioritize your writing tasks, and take them on one at a time.
- [ ] Practice saying "No, I can't do x because I have a deadline." Even if it's a self-imposed one.
- [ ] Plan your writing week in advance, so you're not flying by the seat of your pants or procrastinating.
- [ ] Reward yourself every single time you meet your deadline, no matter how big or small.
- [ ] Make reasonable deadlines. Set yourself up for success.
- [ ] Work when you're most productive. Move heaven and earth to get in writing time during those productive hours.
- [ ] No multitasking! Devote yourself to the singular task at hand.
- [ ] Look for opportunities to have a deadline imposed upon you. For instance, submit a small piece of your writing to a contest. Apply for a writing fellowship where you have to submit sample work. Keep track of your favorite magazines or literary journals or online lit magazines and answer their calls for submissions.
- [ ] List other ideas that have worked for you in the past re. deadlines.

> "Get it down. Take chances. It may be bad, but it's the only way you can do anything really good."
>
> ~William Faulkner

List all the times you have taken something bad and revised it to make it good, or even, really good.

You've done it before—you can do it again!

WRITE BACK!

"I don't sit around waiting for passion to strike me. I keep working steadily, because I believe it is our privilege as humans to keep making things. Most of all, I keep working because I trust that creativity is always trying to find me, even when I have lost sight of it."
~Elizabeth Gilbert

Dear Liz,

_____

_____

_____

_____

_____

_____

_____

_____

_____

_____

Your Fellow Writer, Me

The Inspired Writer

T	E	X	P	R	E	S	S	I	O	N	R	G	E
P	T	Y	T	I	R	A	L	C	T	A	I	G	H
S	L	I	T	E	R	A	R	Y	R	A	N	N	R
E	V	O	I	C	E	S	U	M	V	P	S	I	O
C	R	E	A	T	I	V	E	R	O	U	P	L	H
V	N	O	I	S	I	V	E	R	C	L	I	L	P
R	P	E	E	E	F	H	T	T	A	I	R	E	A
O	R	T	S	L	S	A	G	C	B	T	A	S	T
H	S	A	A	I	L	A	E	I	U	Z	T	T	E
T	E	I	L	E	I	W	N	T	L	E	I	S	M
U	R	B	N	I	O	A	I	E	A	R	O	E	L
A	U	T	I	A	N	R	U	O	R	S	N	B	U
P	H	R	A	S	E	D	S	P	Y	Z	A	O	N
L	C	O	M	P	O	S	E	T	O	O	L	P	E

INSPIRATIONAL
PUBLISHER
CLARITY
VOCABULARY
EASE
AWARDS
REVISION
EXPRESSION
AUTHOR
BESTSELLING
MUSE
METAPHOR
POETIC
PULITZER
LITERARY
GENIUS
CREATIVE
TALENT
COMPOSE
PHRASE
VOICE
FLAIR

Find the answer key in the back of the book.

"Writer's block occurs when a writer has nothing to say. Unfortunately not all writers experience it."

~Ron Brackin

Let's get SNARKY! Name some writers you WISH had writer's block, and why.

Make a list of all the things you are curious about in your current writing project/s.

Make a list of all the things you are curious about in general (maybe you can write about those!)

"One way to deal with writer's block is to walk until a strange flower grows in time-lapse-photography fashion out of your head."

~Evan Fleischer

Take yourself out for a walk, and meditate on your current writing project. See if any flowers grow out of your head. (Be sure to take a pen and paper or your phone or this book with you to take notes!)

WRITE BACK!

"When asked, 'How do you write?' I invariably answer, 'One word at a time,' and the answer is invariably dismissed. But that is all it is. It sounds too simple to be true, but consider the Great Wall of China, if you will: one stone at a time, man. That's all. One stone at a time."

~Stephen King

Dear Stephen,

_____

_____

_____

_____

_____

_____

_____

_____

_____

_____

_____

_____

_____

Your Fellow Writer, Me

"On a writer's path there are always some level of pain and solitude, life and death, love and hate, longing and fullness of soul, romance and separation, contemplation and adventure."

~Frederick Vanderbuilt

Use these two pages to draw your writer's path, from your earliest memories of writing until now. Include your highs and lows, your successes and challenges, your stepping stones and your stumbling blocks, the twists and turns and curves and straightaways, etc.

Imagine your writer's block taking out a personal ad. Write the ad under the photograph.

WRITE BACK!

"You don't start out writing good stuff. You start out writing crap and thinking it's good stuff, and then gradually you get better at it. That's why I say one of the most valuable traits is persistence."

~Octavia Butler

Dear Octavia,

_____

_____

_____

_____

_____

_____

_____

_____

_____

_____

_____

Your Fellow Writer, Me

Imagine your writer's block has died, and write its obituary.

You may have heard of the *5 Love Languages* by Gary Chapman. Here's an adaptation using self-love instead. When you're experiencing a particularly painful bout of writer's block, give yourself some love.

☆The Self-Love Languages

Physical Touch	Things that make your body feel good and focus on your physical wellbeing.	Massages Spa Days Soft Blankets Moving Your Body Skin Care
Acts of Service	Doing things for yourself that make life easier and more structured.	Therapy Organizing Cleaning Scheduling Delegating Planners
Receiving Gifts	Buying gifts for yourself & spending money on things that bring you joy.	Going Out Makeup Vacations Clothes Craft Investing in Supplies Youself
Words of Affirmation	Giving yourself pep talks & encouraging words by being your biggest cheerleader.	Positive Self-Talk Daily Affirmations Journaling Self-Improvement
Quality Time	Spending time alone, time with your hobbies, and doing what you love.	Meditation Reading Hobbies Art Taking yourself on dates

@SelfLoveRainbow | Inspired by the Five Love Languages by Gary Chapman

I can love myself with physical touch by…

I can love myself with acts of service like...

I can love myself with gifts like...

I can love myself with words of affirmation like...

I can love myself with quality time doing things like...

"If your house is clean, you're not writing. . . . How come you had the time to clean your sink? And you did it with so much passion and energy and gusto. How come, huh? Because you weren't writing."

~Nancy Slonim Aronie

List all of your favorite ways to procrastinate, to not-write.

> "You can't think yourself out of a writing block, you have to write yourself out of a thinking block."
>
> ~John Rogers

Write down all the thoughts you are thinking about your current experience of writer's block.

What more empowering thoughts about writing might you think instead?

WRITE BACK!

"I deal with writer's block by lowering my expectations. I think the trouble starts when you sit down to write and imagine that you will achieve something magical and magnificent—and when you don't, panic sets in. The solution is never to sit down and imagine that you will achieve something magical and magnificent. I write a little bit, almost every day, and if it results in two or three or (on a good day) four good paragraphs, I consider myself a lucky man. Never try to be the hare. All hail the tortoise."

~Malcolm Gladwell

Dear Malcolm,

_____

_____

_____

_____

_____

_____

_____

_____

_____

_____

_____

Your Fellow Writer, Me

> "Confront the page that taunts you with its whiteness. Face your enemy and fill it with words. You are bigger and stronger than a piece of paper."
>
> ~Fennel Hudson

You have all the words you need. Fill these two pages with all the words you can think of. No order, no rhyme, no reason—big words, small words, funny words, cuss words, words in pig latin or any language—just get words out of your head and onto the page.

"At the moment someone is writing he is miraculously driven to forget the immediate circumstances of his own life."

~Natalia Ginzberg

What circumstances of your own life do you need to forget right now in order to write? Can you put them inside of this box for now, and come back to them after you've written?

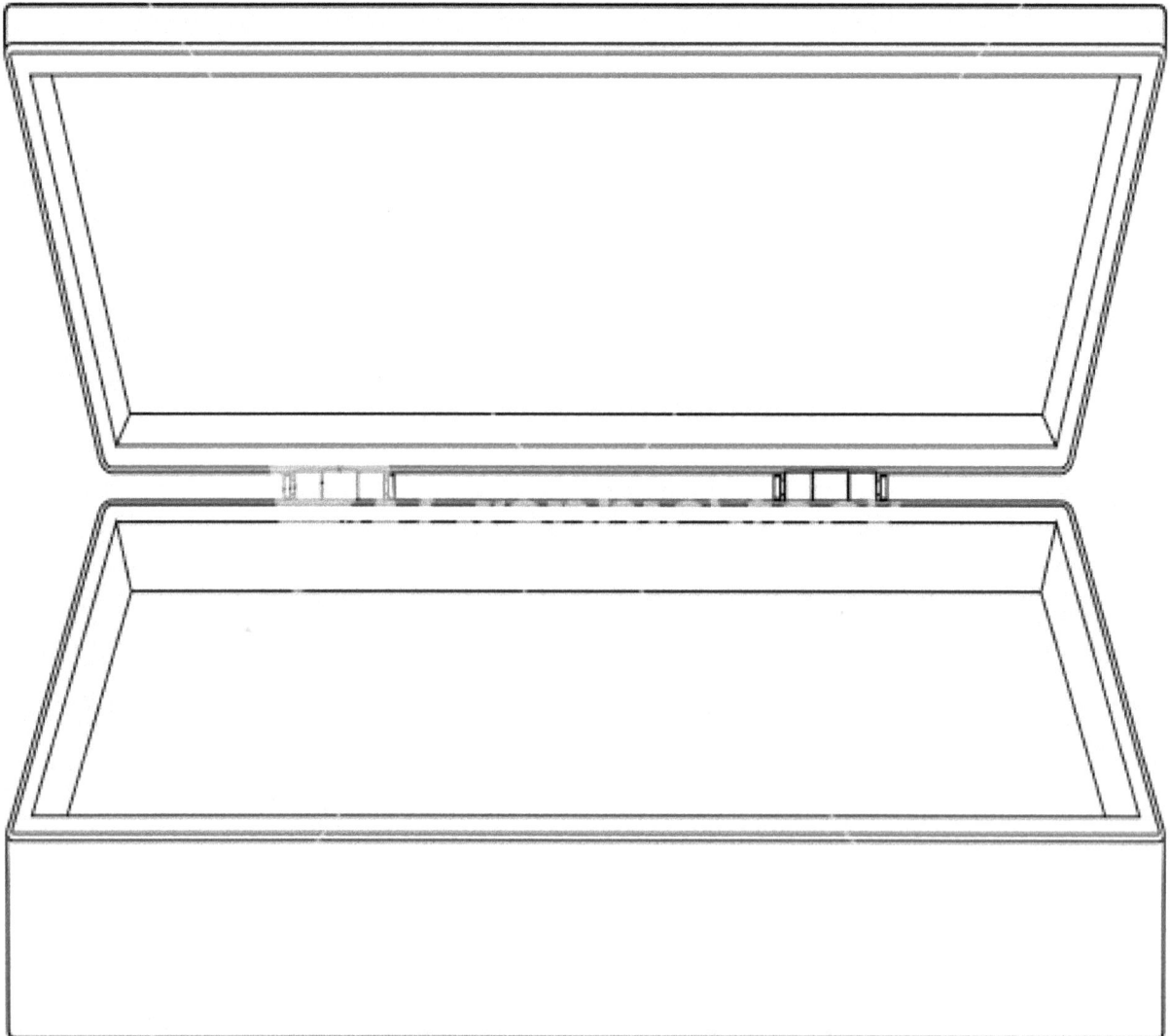

"Writing, like being a good hand with a horse, requires wakefulness and a willingness to surrender."

~Gretel Ehrlich

Surrender (verb): to give up completely or agree to forgo especially in favor of another

What might your writer's block be asking you to surrender?

Ride On!

WRITE BACK!

"A writer is someone for whom writing is more difficult than it is for other people."

~Thomas Mann

Dear Thomas,

_____

_____

_____

_____

_____

_____

_____

_____

_____

_____

_____

_____

_____

_____

Your Fellow Writer, Me

"The problem [with writer's block] is acceptance, which is something we're taught not to do. We're taught to improve uncomfortable situations, to change things, alleviate unpleasant feelings. But if you accept the reality that you have been given—that you are not in a productive creative period—you free yourself to being filling up again."

~Anne Lamott

Lamott suggests to her students that when they are blocked, they write one page, just three hundred words—"memories or dreams or stream of consciousness on how much they hate writing"—and then, "on bad days and weeks, let things go at that."

Ready? Set? GO! Three hundred words. Easy peasy.

We writers are shy, nocturnal creatures. Push us into the light and the light blinds us.

~John Banville

Maybe this is true for you, or maybe not. What kind of a creature are you as a writer? Describe (or draw!) your creaturely self (or selves!) in detail.

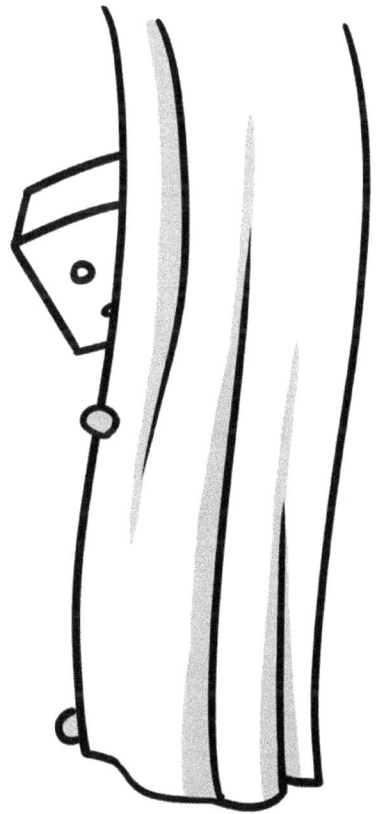

WRITE BACK!

"There is nothing to writing. All you do is sit down at a typewriter and bleed."

~Ernest Hemingway

Dear Ernest,

_____

_____

_____

_____

_____

_____

_____

_____

_____

_____

_____

_____

_____

_____

_____

Your Fellow Writer, Me

GETTING UNBLOCKED!

Find the answer key at the end of the book.

MAD LIBS
WRITER'S BLOCK

Favorite male writer _____

Favorite female writer _____

Grocery store _____

Least favorite color _____

Animal—plural _____

Piece of women's clothing _____

Foul smell _____

Strange animal _____

Comfort food _____

Adverb _____

Male body part _____

Serious occupation _____

Funny occupation _____

Town/city you don't like _____

Number _____

Verb ending in "s" _____

Adverb _____

Gross food _____

Large number _____

Kind of alcohol _____

Verb—present tense _____ (TURN TO NEXT PAGE)

MAD LIBS
WRITER'S BLOCK

One day _____ and _____ met in the
           FAVORITE MALE WRITER   FAVORITE FEMALE WRITER

aisle at _____. His face was _____ and swollen, and his
          GROCERY STORE   LEAST FAVORITE COLOR

breath smelled like _____ had made their home there. She was a mess
                      ANIMAL--PLURAL

herself—her too-tight _____ was looked like it hadn't been washed in
                       PIECE OF WOMEN'S CLOTHING

days, and she smelled like _____. She was pushing a _____
                            FOUL SMELL   STRANGE ANIMAL

in her cart, which was full of dozens of packages of _____ ."Writer's
                                                      COMFORT FOOD

block?" he asked, pointing to her cart. "Yes," she replied _____. "You
                                                             ADVERB

too?" He nodded, rubbing his _____ absentmindedly. "Don't you
                              MALE BODY PART

sometimes wish you were a _____ instead?" he asked. "No," she
                           SERIOUS OCCUPATION

replied. "I'd rather be a _____ who lived in _____
                          FUNNY OCCUPATION   TOWN/CITY YOU DON'T LIKE

with _____ needy children and a husband who _____ poorly than
      NUMBER   VERB ENDING IN "S"

than be a writer right now." He laughed _____. "I get it," he said. "After
                                              ADVERB

I pay for all this _____,I'm heading to the bar to down
                          GROSS FOOD

_____ pints of _____." Now that's a stereotype," she
     LARGE NUMBER   KIND OF ALCOHOL

replied. "If the shoe fits," he said, shrugging his shoulders, "you should

_____ it."
VERB—PRESENT TENSE

> "Your intuition knows what to write, so get out of the way."
>
> ~Ray Bradbury

Write a letter to you from your intuition.

Dear _____,

_____

_____

_____

_____

_____

_____

_____

_____

_____

_____

_____

_____

Love, Your Intuition

"I think there are two types of writers, the architects and the gardeners. The architects plan everything ahead of time, like an architect building a house. They know how many rooms are going to be in the house, what kind of roof they're going to have, where the wires are going to run, what kind of plumbing there's going to be. They have the whole thing designed and blueprinted out before they even nail the first board up. The gardeners dig a hole, drop in a seed and water it. They kind of know what seed it is, they know if they planted a fantasy seed or mystery seed or whatever. But as the plant comes up and they water it, they don't know how many branches it's going to have, they find out as it grows. And I'm much more a gardener than an architect."

~George R. R. Martin

When it comes to your writing type, are you more of a/n (circle one)

Architect   Gardener

How might your writing type be contributing to your current writer's block?

How might trying the opposite type help free you from your current writer's block?

What are some concrete steps you can take to embrace your opposite type?

"A blank piece of paper is God's way of telling us how hard it is to be God."

~Sidney Sheldon

Write a letter to you from an imaginary beleaguered writing-blocked God.

Dear _____,

_____

_____

_____

_____

_____

_____

_____

_____

_____

_____

_____

_____

_____

_____

_____

_____

_____

_____

_____

_____

_____

_____

_____

_____

_____

_____

With empathy, God

> "You get a good review, and it's like crack. You need another hit. And another. And another. I know authors are like Tinkerbell and generally need applause to survive, but it's a slippery slope."
>
> ~Alexandra Bracken

Imagine your current writing project is complete. Do a hit-job on yourself. Write several over-the-top reviews from your ideal reviewers. Throw every superlative in the book into those reviews, and don't forget the exclamation points!!!

"Writing every book, the writer must solve two problems: Can it be done? And, Can I do it?"

~Annie Dillard

Imagine you are in Writer's Court, and the question before the jury is "Can it be done?" and "Can you do it?"

First, make a case for the prosecution, arguing that the answer to both questions is no.

Then, make a case for the defense, arguing that the answer to both questions is yes.

If you were the jury, how would you decide the case?

If you would side with the prosecution, it's time for a retrial!
What else can you add to your defense?

"The only good teachers for you are those friends who love you, who think you are interesting, or very important, or wonderfully funny; whose attitude is: 'Tell me more. Tell me all you can. I want to understand more about everything you feel and know, and all the changes inside and out of you. Let more out.'

And if you have no such friend, —and you want to write, —when then you must imagine one."

~Brenda Ueland

Write a letter from your imaginary friend who believes in you and knows you can crush your writer's block.

Dear _____,

_____

_____

_____

_____

_____

_____

_____

_____

_____

Love, Your Imaginary Friend

"A schedule defends from chaos and whim. It is a net for catching days. It is a scaffolding on which a worker can stand and labor with both hands at sections of time. A schedule is a mock-up of reason and order—willed, faked, and so brought into being; it is a peace and a haven set into the wreck of time; it is a lifeboat on which you find yourself, decades later, still living."

~Annie Dillard

If writing is not your full-time job, do you have a regular writing schedule that you have willed or faked into being? Circle one:

Yes   No   Sometimes

If the answer is yes or sometimes, how does your schedule make you feel? Does it bring you peace, as Annie Dillard suggests? Or?

If the answer is no, why don't you have a schedule? List all your reasons.

Now, try making a writing schedule for the next week. Shade in all the times you'll devote to writing (or staring at the screen not writing, which is writing too!).

Time	Sun	Mon	Tues	Wed	Thurs	Fri	Sat
12:00 am							
1:00 am							
2:00 am							
3:00 am							
4:00 am							
5:00 am							
6:00 am							
7:00 am							
8:00 am							
9:00 am							
10:00 am							
11:00 am							
12:00 pm							
1:00 pm							
2:00 pm							
3:00 pm							
4:00 pm							
5:00 pm							
6:00 pm							
7:00 pm							
8:00 pm							
9:00 pm							
10:00 pm							
11:00 pm							

> "Many fine people were out there living, people whose consciences permitted them to sleep at night despite their not having written a decent sentence that day, or ever."
>
> ~Annie Dillard

Write a letter to one of those fine people who can sleep at night because they don't write, and can't understand why you can't.

Dear Fine Person,

_____

_____

_____

_____

_____

_____

_____

_____

_____

_____

_____

_____

From a Writer, Me

> "Writers end up writing about their obsessions. Things that haunt them; things they can't forget; stories they carry in their bodies waiting to be released."
>
> ~Natalie Goldberg

Writer's block may be a sign you're not obsessed enough with your topic at hand. Is there anything about it that obsesses you?

To prime the pump, write here about something else you are currently obsessed with.

Write here about something from your past that continues to haunt you.

Can you take your obsessions and hauntings and turn them into a new writing project? (Once your current one is done, if need be.)

"Writers are great lovers. They fall in love with other writers. That's how they learn to write. They take on a writer, read everything by him or her, read it over again until they understand how the writer moves, pauses, and sees. That's what being a lover is: stepping out of yourself, stepping into someone else's skin. Your ability to love another's writing means those capabilities are awakened in you."

~Natalie Goldberg

Let's explore your great love affairs with other writers.

Name of Writer	What I Love About Their Writing

Which writers whom you love are you most alike?

Which writers whom you love are most different from you?

Which capabilities of your beloved writers do you most need to awaken right now to move through your writer's block?

> "There is neither a proportional relationship, nor an inverse one, between a writer's estimation of a work in progress and its actual quality. The feeling that the work is magnificent, and the feeling that it is abominable, are both mosquitoes to be repelled, ignored, or killed, but not indulged."
>
> ~Annie Dillard

SYNONYMS FOR MAGNIFICENT	SYNONYMS FOR ABOMINABLE

In all likelihood, your writing may neither be magnificent or abominable. What would be some less pesky mosquito-words that could describe writing you would be proud of, that wouldn't be an over- or an under-indulgence?

THE FIVE STAGES OF WRITER'S BOOK

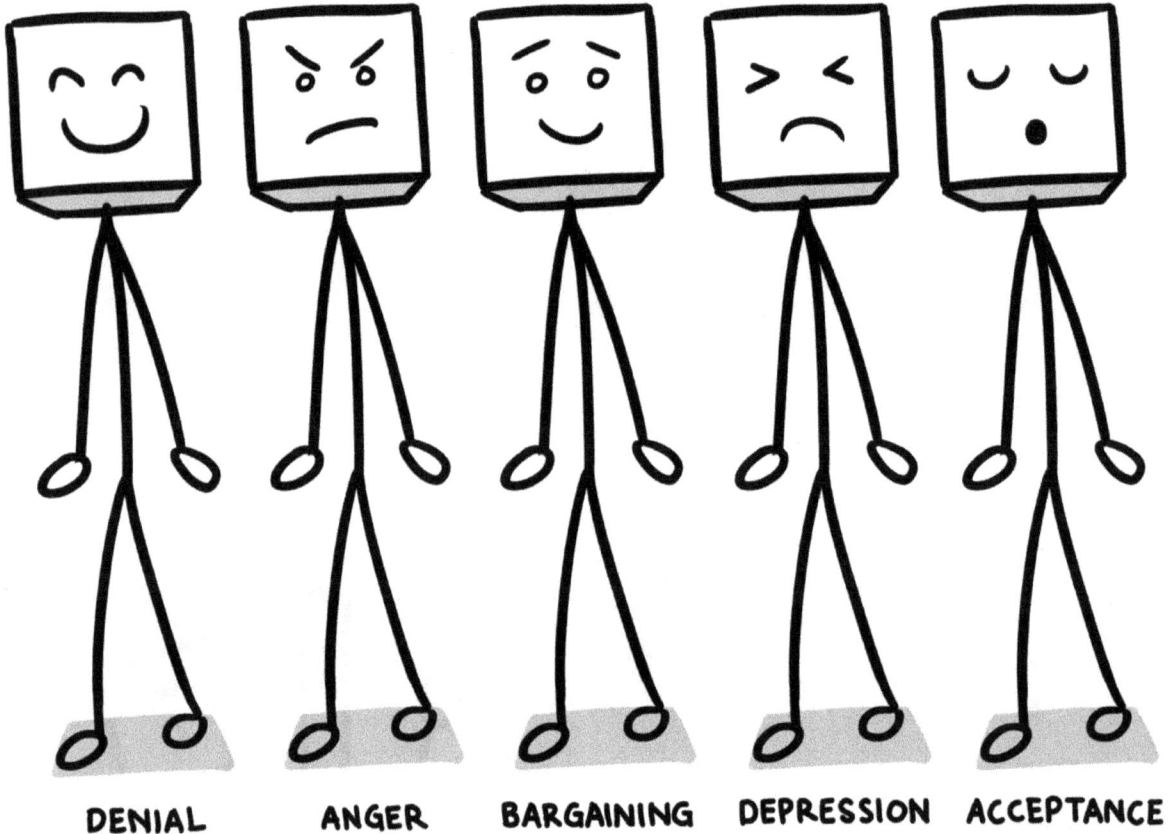

DENIAL · ANGER · BARGAINING · DEPRESSION · ACCEPTANCE

DENIAL: I'm not blocked, I'm just percolating ideas! Or, I could write if I want to. I've just got other stuff going on.

ANGER: ERG! Why is this so freaking hard? Or, ACK! For crying out loud, it's just words. It's ridiculous to be this blocked.

BARGAINING: If I can get past this block and finish X (whatever piece of writing you're blocked on), I promise I'll turn all my attention to Y (whatever person/place/thing you've been neglecting). Or, as soon as I finish this piece of writing, I'll never force myself to write again.

DEPRESSION: This piece is hopeless. I'll never finish it. Or, I'm hopeless. Why bother writing anything? It's not worth it. I'm not worth it.

ACCEPTANCE: Yep, I'm blocked. It happens to the best of writers. What else can I do until this block passes? Or, blocked again! Let me try some tried and true strategies and see if I can loosen this block.

What stage of writer's block are you currently in?

For each of the five stages, write down how they manifest for you. What do you tell yourself in each stage?

DENIAL:

ANGER:

BARGAINING:

DEPRESSION:

ACCEPTANCE:

OH SHIT!

"The first draft of anything is shit."

~Ernest Hemingway

"Shitty first drafts. . . . All good writers write them. This is how they end up with good second drafts and terrific third drafts."

~Anne Lamott

"The perfect is the enemy of the good."

~Voltaire

What are your thoughts about giving yourself permission to write a shitty first draft?

What role might perfectionism play in your writer's block? Is perfectionism the enemy of you being able to write a good second draft or a terrific third one?

> "Writing is a form of therapy; sometimes I wonder how all those who do not write, compose, or paint can manage to escape the madness, melancholia, the panic and fear which is inherent in a human situation."
>
> ~Graham Greene

While it may be true that writing is a form of therapy, it's equally true that sometimes writers *need* therapy, especially when they are blocked.

Imagine your writer's block going to therapy—what would he or she tell the therapist?

How many words can you form from the term "WRITER'S BLOCK"? Go!

("Trick" is one example.)

The Inspired Writer Answer Key

T	E	X	P	R	E	S	S	I	O	N	R	G	E
P	T	Y	T	I	R	A	L	C	T	A	I	G	H
S	L	I	T	E	R	A	R	Y	R	A	N	N	R
E	V	O	I	C	E	S	U	M	V	P	S	I	O
C	R	E	A	T	I	V	E	R	O	U	P	L	H
V	N	O	I	S	I	V	E	R	C	L	I	L	P
R	P	E	E	F	H	T	T	A	I	R	E	A
O	R	T	S	L	S	A	G	C	B	T	A	S	T
H	S	A	A	I	L	A	E	I	U	Z	T	T	E
T	E	I	L	E	I	W	N	T	L	E	I	S	M
U	R	B	N	I	O	A	I	E	A	R	O	E	L
A	U	T	I	A	N	R	U	O	R	S	N	B	U
P	H	R	A	S	E	D	S	P	Y	Z	A	O	N
L	C	O	M	P	O	S	E	T	O	O	L	P	E

The Uninspired Writer Answer Key

C	S	S	P	P	C	L	I	C	H	E	D	S	B
R	U	X	C	E	E	M	P	T	Y	N	D	R	L
Y	O	R	L	E	L	Z	I	L	C	H	P	F	I
T	N	U	N	I	N	S	P	I	R	E	D	B	S
E	I	E	M	L	O	T	R	I	T	E	A	L	T
I	D	H	I	R	O	R	O	P	C	C	T	A	L
X	U	A	M	O	D	D	U	L	L	E	S	N	E
N	T	C	P	I	S	I	E	L	A	T	S	K	S
A	I	K	O	R	D	E	R	O	S	N	E	C	S
Y	T	E	S	E	O	F	E	A	R	F	U	L	D
D	A	Y	T	F	E	E	S	T	U	C	K	L	S
R	L	E	E	N	E	R	C	O	I	D	E	M	E
Y	P	D	R	I	D	U	B	L	O	C	K	E	D
I	D	E	P	R	E	S	S	E	D	T	A	D	M

The Maze Answer Key

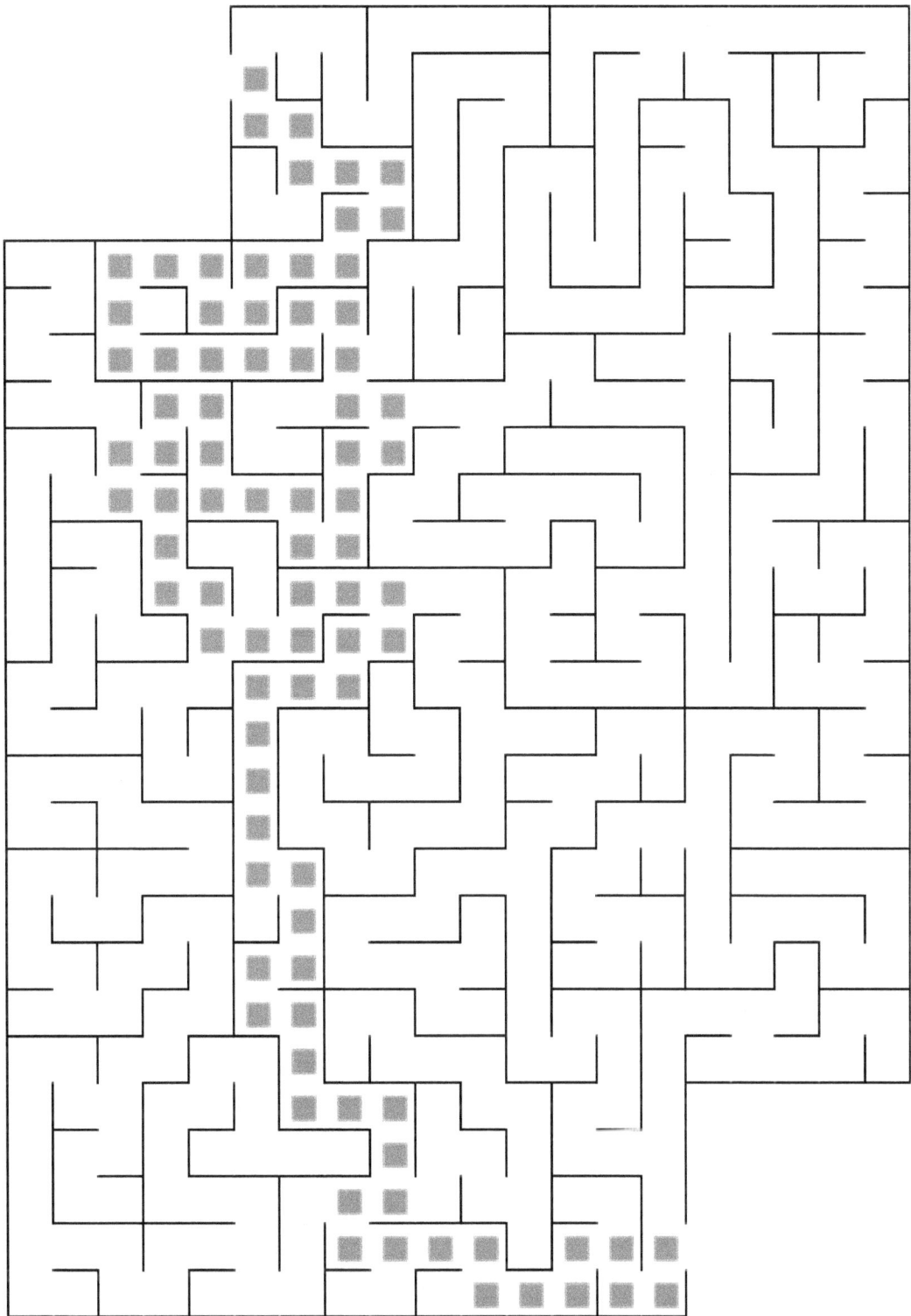

FAMOUR AUTHOR ANSWER KEY

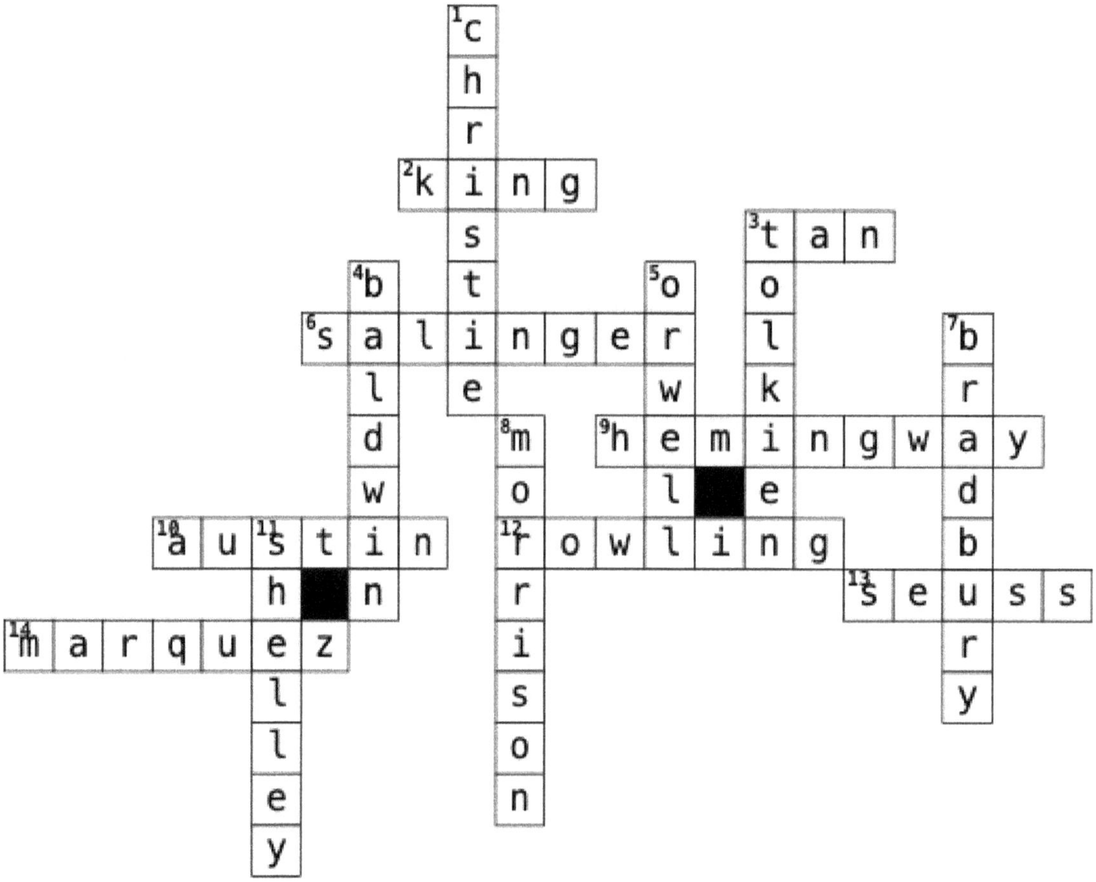
1 christie
2 king
3 tan
3 tolkien
4 baldwin
5 orwell
6 salinger
7 bradbury
8 morrison
9 hemingway
10 austin
11 shelley
12 rowling
13 seuss
14 marquez

Across

2. Misery loves company
3. You'd feel joy if you joined her lucky club
6. Catch him in the rye
9. Nicknamed Papa
10. Pride or prejudiced?
12. A famous potter maker
13. Red fish blue fish
14. A century of solitude

Down

1. Murder she wrote
3. It's all about the ring
4. Be careful of the fire next time
5. Farm animals
7. Books are burning at 451 degrees
8. She's beloved
11. She created a monster

ABOUT THE AUTHOR

Jennifer Leigh Selig, PhD, has been a prolific writer since she first picked up a #2 Ticonderoga pencil. She is the author of several dozen newspaper articles, book reviews, and essays; she has completed three screenplays; she's either written, edited, or contributed to twenty books, and she owns three publishing imprints dedicated to helping writers fulfill their dreams of becoming authors. As a writing teacher for thirty-five years of over two thousand students, she's seen her share of writer's block. But it wasn't until she was writing her doctoral dissertation in her late 30s that she experienced a nearly debilitating bout of it herself. The block was so bad that she told her friends and family (who were completely dismissive of her pain, given her prolific history of writing) that if she had known how hard it was to write a dissertation, she wouldn't have pursued a doctorate in the first place.

She did finish it, and earned her PhD in psychology. She brings her wise and witty first-hand knowledge of writer's block to this book.

Dr. Selig's other books include:

Deep Creativity: Seven Ways to Spark Your Creative Spirit
Everyday Reverence: A Hundred Ways to Kneel and Kiss the Ground
Integration: The Psychology and Mythology of Martin Luther King, Jr. and His (Unfinished) Therapy With the Soul of America
Re-Imagining Education: Essays on Reviving the Soul of Learning
Re-Ensouling Education: Essays on the Importance of the Humanities in Schooling the Soul

Find her at www.jenniferleighselig.com
Visit her publishing imprints at:

Mandorla Books—www.mandorlabooks.com
Empress Publications—www.empresspublications.com
Grace's Giant Print Books—www.gracesgiantprintbooks.com

WRITE BACK!

Tell Jennifer what was most useful about this book.

Dear Jennifer,

_____

_____

_____

_____

_____

_____

_____

_____

_____

_____

_____

_____

_____

Your Fellow Writer, Me

www.ingramcontent.com/pod-product-compliance
Lightning Source LLC
Chambersburg PA
CBHW052116020426

42335CB00021B/2788